First paperback edition September 2019

www.facebook.com/KellieBbooks

Written by Kellie Ann Briseno M.Ed

Illustrations and Formatting by Ros Webb

ISBN 978-1-6906-0957-5 (paperback)

ISBN 978-0-5785-7205-5 (hardcover)

In loving memory of Robert Lewis Reynolds Sr.
The foundation of an amazing family.

Francesca
Finds Her Father

Kellie Ann Briseno M.Ed
Illustrated By Ros Webb

Francesca's mother never talked about Dad. There weren't any pictures of him around the house. There were no fond memories to treasure and if he stood right in front of her, Francesca would not recognize him.

Still, Francesca often wondered about her father. "Was he tall and strong like Grandpa?", she would ask. But Mom never gave much to go by.

One afternoon, Francesca's friend invited her to the park to play ball. "My dad's taking me to the park. Would you like to come?", asked Francesca's friend. "Certainly!", Francesca said with a grin. She was eager to join them because she figured this would be the perfect opportunity to find a father just like her friend's.

When they got to the park, Francesca looked around and saw plenty of fathers. There were fathers playing tennis and fathers pushing their children on the swings. Fathers were absolutely everywhere! But much to her disappointment, Francesca's father was not there. She realized that all the fathers had already had their own children to play with. So, Francesca decided to search elsewhere.

A few days later, Francesca's mom took her to the movies. Although Francesca adored spending time with Mom, there was always something missing. Always a certain void. So, this time she was determined. She continued her quest to find her father.

When they arrived, Francesca was once again disappointed. She tried looking up and down each row, but unfortunately, the theater was so dark, she couldn't find her father anywhere. "Well…", she thought to herself. "I guess I'll try again some other time."

Then, Francesca had an idea. She had seen some ads on TV mention that Father's Day would be celebrated in a few weeks. Eureka! Father's Day is especially made for fathers. If Francesca were to find her father any day, she would most definitely find him on Father's Day.

As the days passed, Francesca's anticipation grew stronger. Waiting for Father's Day was almost as intense as waiting for Christmas. On the night before the special day, Francesca laid out her outfit and wrapped up her hair before climbing into bed. She wanted to look really nice if she were to find her father for the first time.

Francesca didn't sleep a wink that night. She stared at the ceiling. Her eyes were wide open as her mind filled with ideas of what it would be like to meet her father. "I wonder if he loves me."

Eventually Francesca fell asleep. When she woke up the next morning, she sprung out of bed and swiftly began to get ready for the day. After eating breakfast, she took a shower, then put on her favorite dress. "Mom, today is Father's Day!", she said with a smile.

She and Mom stopped by the grocery store before heading home from church. As the day carried on, her enthusiasm began to dwindle. It started to seem as if Father's Day was just another Sunday.

Once they got home, Francesca went straight to her room. "Maybe I don't have a Father.", she thought to herself. "Maybe this whole idea was just plain silly". She rested her head in the pillow and before long, she dozed off into a nap.

When she woke up, her mother was waiting patiently at the door. Mom noticed Francesca's enthusiasm about meeting her father and she decided it was about time to introduce them.

Mom handed Francesca a book and began reading a few key passages. Even as Francesca listened, she still didn't quite understand. "You see, your Father was with you when you played ball at the park. He was at the movie theater. He's even here with you on Father's Day. Your Father is always with you.", explained Mom.

Francesca couldn't describe the feeling, but her heart was suddenly filled with love. For some reason, Francesca felt complete. Just then, it dawned on her. Her Father had been with her all along. There was no need to keep looking. The search was over. Francesca had finally found her Father.